# THE PRICK OF LASS

## THE PAINS

SUMEET KUMAR

ISBN 979-888546060-6

*Sumeet Kumar*

**Sumeet Kumar** , A adult who experiences many phases of love in his life , get broked many times , stands up every time and keep moving to the next phases of the life.In reality he is a writter as well as singer (as a hobby).

Very exciting and interesting fact about him is that he is aauthor of New era i.e. he starts his journey of writing at the age when he was going to schools to get the study.His some famous works i.e. Maturity Of Love (Genre - Love),Privacy For Dream (Genre - Middle Class), Army Squad ofLove (Genre- The Seperation of Army Love), 5 Days of Love(Genre- Temporarily Love), Th e Endearment Of Love(Genre - Historical Era Of Love), Social Destruction Indo-Pak (Genre - The Story of The Love At The Time Of Division Of India And Pakistan), Middle Class Soul (Genre - The Dreams of Middle Class), The Accursed Kanatpur (Genre -The Horrific Story Of A Village), Wrong Number (Genre -The Suspenseful Physco Killer Story), The Secrecy OfDeadly Midnight (Genre - The Suspense About a Crime),Fragile Religious Of Death (Genre- The Death Of A TrustfulPerson), Nature Vs Science (Genre - The Future Battle Between Nature And Science In A Horrific Way), Generic Man (Genre - The Dream of I.I.T), The Unconsious 12 Hours(Genre - The Illusion At Stage Of Comma), The StrangeBurden (Genre - The Burden Of Love) , Her Existence (Genre- The Female Pain In The Society) , Jockstrap Prize (Genre -The True Story Of A National Athlete) , H Man [Hindi] (Genre - Superhero Tragic Story), H Man [English] (Genre - Superhero Tragic Story) , Maturity Of Love [Englsih] (Genre - Love). are available on various geners on the offcial platform of **Amazon, Flipkart and Notionpress**. You can buy them from there.

# Contents

*Preface* *vii*

*Acknowledgements* *xiii*

*Prologue* *xv*

1. The Female Child Matricide 1

2. The Juvenile 5

3. The Pain (la Blessés) 9

4. The Ending Of Dreams 13

5. The Demise Of World 16

6. The Pinpointing Of Goddess 19

7. The Inception Of New Entity 23

8. Sternely 26

The Egalitarianism 29

# Preface

Women's are the roots of any family because the always stuffer unity, causes of happiness the have a power of control that child's birth and the most important thing about the women may hide any type of pain when it comes on her family happiness. The have also a passion to complete his dream but the drop it only for his family happinesses. In Now Days Women's Are Not Stood As A Gender Because If They Seen, Them They Are Always Some Of Sacrifice, doing household And The Always Saved Their Family From The Bad Situation And Bad Attempts By Then true Undefined In My Opinion Women Are Human The

Life Of Undefined Whose Single Earth. If we discussed about the women's pan then most of the pain to her is intended to society judgment.( written want to give undefined example on women's pain. don't wear this and under type of clothes , only cook food , Very few chances of studies). Save daughter and educated daughter , it has become just a slogan in today's people because if this is true then there are so many rape cases, Harassment, Abusing, Murder cases, Tourture cases, these never happen undefined nowadays a human everything Forget it, if a girl is raped or accidentally killed, then people will regret it for a few days, after that they will march candles and in the end will fight for some days to get justice undefined after that, if they get the punishment, then the right characters will say that we have tried that very much. Who did not get him to get justice undefined Did you really try to get justice, not at all undefined Because at the time when those genes pass through many problems, the pain they feel, no one can know, can not understand undefined It is from millions Even more how is the spending, more than thousands do not get justice and how many gifts are there who remain silent because of their family undefined From school to college to office, everywhere there is some kind of a scoundrel who is just a curse for the whole society undefined Harrash a girl and at all there was no health because she is afraid of things, not at all undefined She hides that because of this many harm to my family undefined To tell the truth, it is not a pain to understand, there is no man standing in the disguise of man undefined undefined We who see all this, but still remain silent undefined because they never want us to face any trouble or anything to our family. I can't help it, don't ever do any false drama, so that your inner soul also curses you undefined Wrong No one even saved Draupadi's shame, just kept watching and waiting for the time, kept silent because of their religion, they were all wrong undefined They were all equally responsible as the rest of the people undefined Sometimes more than the perpetrator of the crime, watching her happen The one who is guilty is undefined already sold undefined but you don't ever do this undefined stay is no easy thing we have to fight together because we are so this is the whole world if not us then no one undefined if your daughters your sisters or any If the girl wants to get justice, then we have to fight ourselves, get justice ourselves, and never give death to the poor because they will dare again to do all this undefined and we will again lose someone's daughter again. Will give undefined and the family members who remain silent and do not say what to them even after all this is very guilty because all the time they think of such an understanding which has never been brewed for them when its need was undefined May someone need it today I am not talking nor am writing someone's story because it is a fact of every man's house in which there is a girl (one sister, one mother, one daughter undefined undefined how many articles, there are books, how many advertisement come But we read it for a while and see it and then forget it if undefined If I want to change my mind then change my mind undefined If I want to save my daughters and sisters from the poor, then end their nest....Nowadays people in the world have started thinking so much about themselves that they should never The pain of others does not seem to be undefined, it is not cured by seeing the pain, by sharing them undefined these toh rapes cases, now there is a lot as if the tourism system has heard undefined, they never get pain from their loved ones, they care about us undefined what age at which age I have shown a girl how to play with toys, how she should take care of her relationship undefined age in which she should have pens and books in her hands, how to make husband happy in her age and how to live with her undefined tour system Its name should not be, its name should be that how any girl's life is splattered, how she gives pain in young age, how her whole childhood is splattered, how to imprison her like five undefined daughters, assuming business So when he is handed over to someone undefined then why not make a boy a business. Their studies, their future, why do they seem to be moving forward, our understanding is visible to us. defined Everyday we see some woman, girl, daughter sister demanding justice, but we keep silent even after hearing that voice outside the four dibaros undefined If there is no relation then what will not be handled, by the way, it is not yours till today's time. Until then he does not give any support to undefined for the right reason why do you later say that it is wrong, it is wrong. Because the biggest mistake we have made is undefined

"

***"Not be a participant in the crime***
***but saw the crime***
***you don't consider yourself wrong***
***because you didn't have a hand in it***
***But those eyes were....***
***Every time a girl has a voice***
***I am a woman, it does not mean that you should curse me***
***I am a woman it does not mean that you took away my childhood from me***
***I'm a girl, it doesn't mean that I have to follow a***

***man at the time***
***Because you also started with us and ended with us..."***"

# ACKNOWLEDGEMENTS

***AMAN KUMAR***

Special Thanks to **Aman Kumar** who worked so hard in the preparation of this book. He has continually put with my passive voice, omission of words, and late night calls. You have be en wonderful. Thanks to him for his precious time in reviewing proposals , individual chapters and early drafts, along with his suggestions on the applicability of the material to the world.

# Prologue

Women are not weak, want to beat their weakness and want to study and educate their daughters as much. Our. It's not a matter of bash. Only a woman can do this, only a mother can do it, only a wife can do it.. A girl leaves her everything and comes, name identity , her happiness, her dream, even her habit to the parents But... still people says that apart from doing household chores, what have you done in life.. I don't know how many women are independent now and how many are not. Because the ratio still says that whatever they are It is very less.... as much as the world is wrong, we all have to blame for one woman only.. like.. if someone's husband got murdered and he got new marriage, then people will take luck at the right time. Don't consider it wrong because even people consider a woman wrong even at the time....why???? If we can't handle the pain that a mother has to bear for nine months till we give birth, we never accept any woman again. Rate not given......

"

***"In whose lap we played***<br>
***he damn him today***<br>
***Girl becomes mother***<br>
***he is denying it today......."***
"

# I

# The Female Child Matricide

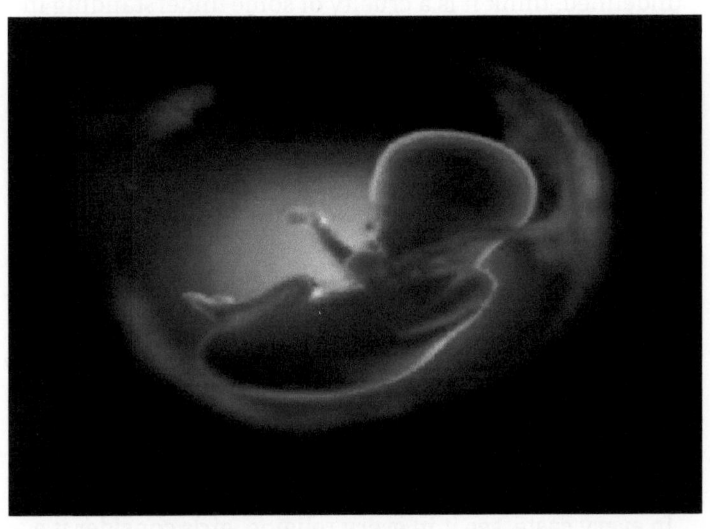

The Female Child Murder has the same meaning as everyone knows these days, it is not just a word, it is a freedom, it is undefined for today's understanding that if a woman in someone's family gave birth to a girl, then that If she grows up, she will marry her at a young age I will not be able to leave the story bye too karnachahu then because there are so many cases in the world related to them that even counting is not a matter of anyone's bash undefined take only a few 20 years 10millions of new born babies are killed undefined is the same reason all undefined I never discriminate against anyone, why I know this very well, if I want to be like her, I will not be able to be like her undefined If it is wrong to be a girl, then a relationship like a mother should be called a relationship like sister Yes, because somewhere or the other, she is also a girl. It is undefined, think it is a cruelty of some understanding in people who become a poison (poison) when a woman gives birth to a girl undefined Where we worship Maa Lakshmi, Maa Durga, Maa Saraswati we worship Maa Kali. Why do this crime in the country is undefined, I know that today, many people will log against what is being written, they will refuse to accept it and will say that this is not completely true at all. .. what is the desire to get a boy or to grow your lineage with him, you become a killer arrow, while forgetting, you also have the foundation of the same bricks which once called a girl, a woman is called one, mother is called hai ekbehen says and you can never describe so many relationships in your own words undefined nowadays look in every house even if you see it in every caste, see it in every religion, girls consider it a burden undefined because they are like your son to others Pagandi cannot be seen, therefore, why is it worth wandering around everywhere and abusing girls? This is not undefined topic (not only the topic is undefined May who am writing these things, I am also a boy, I am also a man but I have never done such a thing, leave the mind of undefined undefined the day if I thought notoh my nafsushi Dayesh will leave the body and later only this dead body will be left and nothing else undefined If I talk about the government, then there is nothing in their hands the way we forget humanity and think about ourselves everywhere, just like they have the same work as their own. Think about it. Then why later say that this government is doing wrong, it should not be done like this, it should be made at the place where it is undefined, there is no need to change the understanding because you also have an understanding inside you. To say that I have to change my understanding undefined By sitting in the house, reading so many different types of news articles, we always think that this is a daily thing undefined why it is not your daily, even after reading it, you have especially your heart and soul. Get out of your mind as if you don't care but undefined is right That no one should be behind him until trouble comes on his own undefined Toh stay like this undefined Sometimes even a woman is compelled to kill her child because Vajanti is such an impotent that if her daughter is a child If I don't come in the world, then it will become a coin for these men, I am already impotent in this society. I am wrong even then. I never get any kind of justice in such a crime. Because the log never considers it a crime. It is considered an honor and nothing else. That when no female will remain in the world, then the breed of a man will grow further.

*"“Women are part of honor*
***Not a part of burden.***

***Eager to progress the breed***
***I'm sorry for our luck***
***doing a deal***
***the daughters we curse***
***aspires to be crowned."***”

# II

# The Juvenile

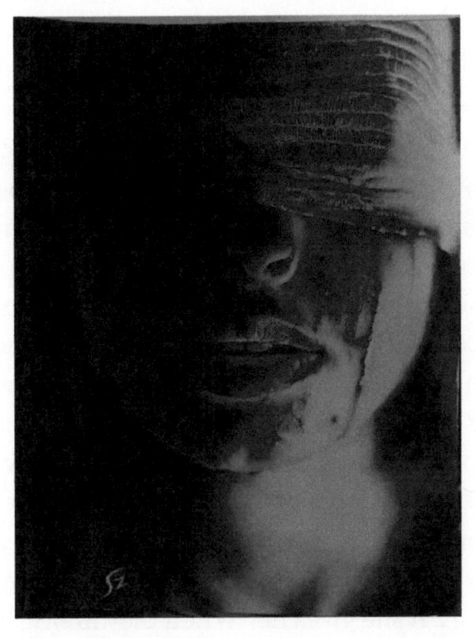

It is very easy to explain the meaning of the teenager of part of a female. Because the biggest dark side if any girl is there then it is . She should wear what? she is talking to those boys whom she meets every day, what is she doing this night, she is being asked. No. If a girl's period is going on, then she does not leave the house for 14 days, there is no sunlight, no shadow, stay in the city and get out somewhere. What has happened: Maybe it's a curse. and sometimes its goes to such an extent that she locks herself in a lonely room. And whatever the problem she can never talk to a man because she knows that nothing will happen Menstrual cycle and periods undefined this is not a thing at all Even after some time, it seems that it is only a mistake. What is the mistake in this that the world sees them in such a way that their whole body is a curse. What is the point of hesitation because this is a natural change of hormones, why keep it hidden from the world, every time you say to the world that you are right or wrong, even if it looks at you with the wrong eyes. It's a human being, it's all wrong, it's not a mistake to stay silent after seeing a crime. And sometimes it happens that only a woman does not understand any other woman. Let's give an example. There are also peoples in many places in the cities who only tell their son to read but not the daughters because because everyone has believed. That she will do after reading that she has to go to another house in the fence, it would have started with such a thing that we are abusing Harrashment Acid Attacks Sexual Violence Partner Violence and there are many such troubles which are due to not reading the beginning .. if she gives her When they are right on time and never do anything about anything, they don't change, so whatever happens with them going forward doesn't happen to a great extent. Barati Padhaobhi is a word.if we talk about today reports (Globally estimated 736 millions women almost one in three-have been subjected to intimate partner violence non partner sexual violence both other least once in her old life 30 parent of vaon aged) ... it's not just the Violence Against Women report, it's the whole world It is the truth of the day which is not visible in today's circles. His own family also speaks at the same time that what did you go to do when he lives, but at the same time you pass by the locality, if you meet him next time, look at him courage. Why??? Ho Jayenge? No at all, if you want to be silent, then you will have to consider yourself a weak mat, man because if you had slapped the boy at the happy time to speak the right to everyone again and again, then he would never try again and that people and the Society is explaining to you, nor do they tell you to stay away from him. Any person can only show you the way, you should come yourself and walk. And the next time someone looked at you, then learn to fight yourself, think of it. You are weak because when you can move forward after bearing the pain of 9 months, then those poor people are so nameless anyway, you toh them I will only say that you can protect your society by yourself and no one should always think that someone will come to help, this world is deserted and this whole society is a lie.. ) We want to meet your needs and go ahead with you ours not ...............

***"If Humanity Ka Marasim"***
***is human power***
***Then you are the producer of humanity***
***and in today's time***
***You are not just a sister, not a mother***
***rather be a whole world of everyone................"***

”

# III

# The Pain (La blessés)

Adhira, a name which means power (power) Her mother is very difficult to face because at the time she herself was facing the exhibition, it is called crisis,hunger in simple words. Her family was thinking that if a girl is born then she should also be born for 13, 15 years, but if a boy is born So he can do whatever he says, because he is a symbol of the progress of the lineage. When Adheera was born, there was no happiness in her family next to her, sad that her father was also whispering that the boy would have been born if the boy was born. And our business would go ahead ... even to the extent that his beating made him feel like a better time than seeing his story. It was going on everywhere that a girl has been born in Keenath's house..By the way, the result of her father was Birju Nath..Adheera's father and mother both were passing through a time and with a condition because the society's thinking has changed. Made them so much that they did not even ask their sweetheart to see the gross of the little one. Hiding that a girl was born in our house. It is only their parents give a difference that if a boy is born then they were made to get it done, if a girl is done, then they will marry her directly before 15 years and send her to their home. There was no manna to marry her as soon as she is 14 years old.. And even if a girl was taught, it is not because she should go ahead and do her dreams. Have got the right.. not at all... Nothing comes. That's why his father thought that he would read it a little. It never happens.. I don't have anything about her childhood. Even if I had my eyes, this heart doesn't know what to say to these alphabets, undefined, so I'm going to tell you from time immemorial, from where it started....something even before that. I want to tell.. Birju Nath's house became impatient, then only his daughters were born, due to which he felt that our feast has increased undefined, so he used to say that the Inkishaadis should be done soon.. We are forced to give a new job to our future. The same thing happened even when Adheera's family saw Adheera's plight, then they realized that we are also wrong. And this was the reason too. And this was also the reason due to which they did not marry their two daughters after the age of 14 years. Why did it come to know only after his departure that no girl should not like a banquet, nor should we ever support them in a banquet in a crime like child marriage in the front of society because it is the only crime whose punishment is found even after death. .Because karma is there for everyone, how can it not be ruined in life for his family...after that, as soon as Adheera passed the $10^{th}$ board exam, his father thought that the time has come..let's do lunch deal.(someone) Man told me that marriage at half of the age of girls is not the reason for our happiness but our compulsion) So I tell them to say that why should we not do the marriage of the ladies???? Why boys are not banquet, so it is some other thing, maybe it will be They are not strangers like girls..why isn't it... Or is he not himself..the society has made his dream China from him and not he himself.. to understand that he has broken every one of his hopes and not he himself.

"

***"With the name of a compulsion***<br>
***Why you send off girls***<br>
***It's not your servent, it's your life***<br>
***Took the pride of the courtyard,***<br>
***now you also consider me as a daughter***<br>
***close my deal***

***I am daughter even though your are right,***
***I am not a stranger,***
***It's no matter how you treat me or burn me***
***But she will not be able to live***
***because you are in yourselves and my soul lives***
***insides in you***
***I am stuck in you"***"

# IV

# The Ending Of Dreams

When adhira turned 14, her marriage took place in a house whose limits were weak from all sides, so it was even worse for everyone. Because there were also boys who did not even say self-pity because their father had a good job and a lot of profession Also, even his own house, which Adheera's father did not have.. When they talked about marriage, Adheera's in-laws talked about dowry, in which they asked for a motorbike and some jewelery and many more from them... For a father where he treats his own child as a feast ..the hatred for him is right . Why does not the relationship go on.. A father's own child turns into a sushi day when he goes to some other house.. On this day he loses himself. Such enmity is making khokla from the rotten coadir of the society nowadays. And we are only seeing it getting hollow..

"

***"If you do desires of graveyard***
***first of all, the logger has gone to his soul,***
***then it is okay otherwise get buried..."***"

On this day only his hope does not break his dream, he lost even six to move forward He also forgot the experience of winning the next generation of force... It is said that every victory is a gift of luck, but when he himself has not only left his lap, how can he say that it is all the gifts of luck. ....well talking about luck, so let's see the fate of Adheera also, what happened to her next, she has become impatient after killing her dreams, let's also see this ... Was that now there is nothing .. no further destination nor any destination bash where life takes you to learn to walk with it .. he left to pursue himself, he had decided his own destination in childhood, till that time Now a prison had been made for him.. He gave up even the desire to speak and the desire to move forward was not weak. talk too was happening at her husband's house..whatever her husband said, she would Nothing else... It is said that fire is such a thing that everyone becomes pure by choosing it, but if it were true, then at that time, after giving a fire test to the mother Sita we worship, I took a holy woman .. but when this society is not pure then how can I make someone else pure... That fire was neither a sieve to his honor, nor his inner soul nor his heart, by feeling it and moving forward. ..if the solution of something is not found with time, then it becomes a pain by going into the bud, which not only harms itself, but in the future also becomes a poison for its own breed.. If she had raised her voice in front of your father..... in front of your in-laws...

***““Time has supported us,***
***but the time has come for us,***
***and the gathering who has refused to tell today***
***my identity,***
***also says to us that you are our life.....”***

# V

# The Demise Of World

It is said that the condition of a woman can only be a woman's society. (Like the drying of a pond and its disposal is with a thirsty, just like a woman is like another woman's society.) Adheera's mother-in-law knew this thing. It's and patient's life ended like this in the school, while working in the house, but I will not allow my future race to end without his profession..whatever is our past, it will never become the future of our race...that That's why she was speaking because she would not be too much of an impatient pregnant woman, she would be about 17 years old when she gave birth to a little girl like her. It means the beauty of the morning, I think it was such a new morning, because of which Adheera has believed that she will live her whole life... Her buds will then be the same things as happened at the time of Adheera's birth. That Adheera's girl has happened There has been a girl of impatience. In today's time, where there is news, in those days, the clothes that used to be side by side also used to work as news and new things too. Used to make.. Adheera was also something happy new because she knew that the society who gave her dreams empty, she should go ahead and kill her daughter's dreams. So it didn't happen at all because at that time his mother-in-law was with him and she had also told him that as long as I stay, your children will not have any problem, I will never let them lose their business, this is me from you. It is also said that there is no happiness or even a limit. This convey kept on going on. They performed their vows. There also came a time when they broke the enclosure done with impatience ... that's because a boy was born in their house. , so the identity, which she used to tell Ahana to get, now she used to tell her grandson (Grandson) to get it, she used to say more than that to him, something to do .

***"What this time has considered as its own***
***the same nowadays***
***identity became the address***
***Some moments are like memories which suddenly***
***disappears."***

After giving birth to a boy, such a Jaish is celebrated as if he has conquered the whole world.. But when a daughter is born a girl, there is nothing left except to call her a disgrace. How will this society celebrate me toh celebration....after that what happened was what was expected. Adheera and her mother-in-law's mother's full attention was now on her son and grandson, by the way, her name was named Dars... The demand was fulfilled immediately and when Ahana asked for something, it was told that you have not made it worth it, is it only for your brother... She was also given due to education because she was not a son, she did not take birth as a boy..after this slowly doing Ahana lost her identity but for some time even though the breed was half keep but like her It was not at all... she had raised his voice, but at the time when that crime had already happened .

# VI

# The Pinpointing Of Goddess

I had expressed it earlier in my alphabets that women's are the root of the family, if they do, then both their breed's physique and disease are destroyed. He had got a lot of work time to see the happiness of your grandson because god had sent the message of death like hell. Whenever his companions were studying, whatever they asked for, she would take them in a short time. He also did the same in childhood, so he was also doing what his father did in childhood. Should have met earlier, in the form of a child, now Vaders was getting what he should have met, now he should be able to see the audience. It seemed that she was suffering, now she was getting her brother Darsh. Can't do it and today it is the biggest crime in Kalkejam.

"

***"I am your heart, you are making yourself jealous by listening to the songs of others.. opponent is my journey with me, your smile is enough to make my world away from my world.***

***""***

When ahana was born, no one had come to see him at that time, neither his maternal grandparents nor any family. Because of the reason he felt that his sighing his daughter is nothing more than a curse for him, when he tried to kill him by poison. She didn't have to give life so why brought her up for nine months???? What was going on in Adheera's heart and mind at that time, perhaps no one knew about it except her. No one came to see, so it was also a matter of fact that her husband was not with her at the time, because as the members of their family were growing up, they also thought that sitting at home would not last the family. Because how many people can feed on a pension, that too a person undefined Ahana's grandfather was a retired government officer and at that time his salary was also a lot of work, due to which he used to go home, but everyone's studies are not completed in him. That's why his father went out somewhere to earn money from him..... Where was his line of handwriting and death decoration in the hands of Susparvalle..

***" smile is the only one who walks on the path of his glory. May God say that this gardener is say something ,***

***Guru Gobind Singh is also the master of the universe, who made our streak.."***

After a year, Ahana's grandmother died because she had typhoid at some point but this was not the reason for her death and the reason was such people also say that I have never heard or heard about it. Ehi last journey for Khushika Darshana till her grandmother is with her now what will happen after this now see for yourself.....

"

***"Existence house has gone,***
***let's say goodbye to the child,***
***and the girl child, whatever the friends are,***
***I prayed to God, my loved ones,***
***if you can, let it all be erased..."***"

# VII

# The Inception Of New Entity

A New Beginning Story which has written its destiny on past.. In the new way the face of different types of troubles is always there. Thinking got attached. took a new journey with your children, a new beginning to move forward ... that the cities where mother Ganga is flow everywhere (Banaras). Lasted for 3 months. Came .. was a relative of a lot of trouble, also came in search of work because at that time he also did not have any work, he also talked to impatience, there is work in your eyes So you give me the money in return for this, I will pay for your children. At that time, they were very desperate for money and the future of their own children. That's why Adheera got her work. But it is said that neither we saved our lives from outsiders If a scoundrel comes in me, how will he save his life from him. She did not know nor for her children ... when her household was not being maintained that she also thought that I also have to do some work now because her husband did not give her a single penny at that time undefined so she did many small things She struggled every day to take care of her own children, that her family should somehow get out of trouble, now she used to say that her children. Hope they should get a good platform for them too, whose flight is much bigger than the society caste. .and they say that you will say no to advance, you will be able to do it yourself.. Now some happy moments also came because from his profession, he used to go to the house of Kanchal and his relative who used to study him because of his profession was also an aspect.. at the time. The condition started getting better as well. And his relatives also. By the way, the society was not silent even at that time because even if a person is a relative, they make log talk. He keeps the other man close to you, he has left the shame. Adheera could not see anything at the time, but at the time, he was only predicting his children and nothing bash was saying to come out of these troubles which he was suffering from many years. ..man should not say anything so much that he harms himself ..these lamps will not come to the society yet. And soon all the secrets will be revealed on this undefined

*"“Smile had one*
*of new words*
*but in return*
*I am in trouble*
*we got some moments*
*and there was hope*
*that this world will make a new revelation*
*But regret we have of this sentence that*
*we can't able to understand at that time ....*
*and the present scenario is the scenario of my*
*death............"*

***Pain, regret, guilt, we come to know about this relationship only when we touch our destination and stay cashless, where stopping is also an enmity with God........"***

# VIII

## Sternely

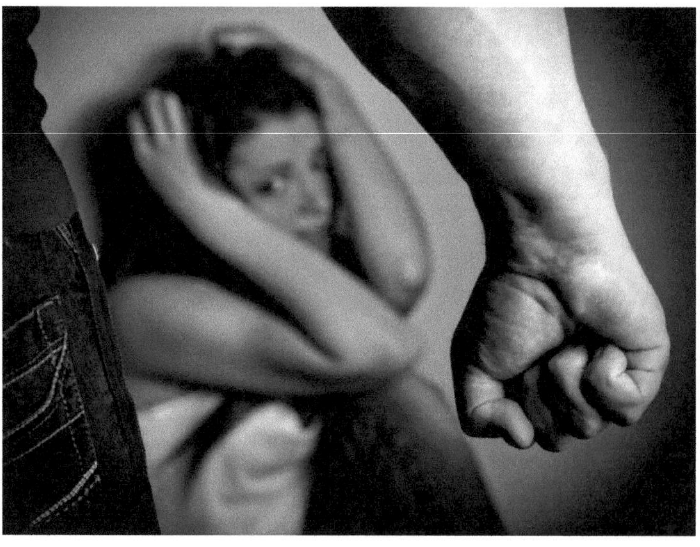

Aahna never realized that the person whom she considers more than her mother and father to feel secure with her, she will one day turn out to be a poor, nor did

Adheera ever realize that the person she has helped, the poor people she cares for. She has been in her own house, her daughter will be destroyed Know ) This continuous cycle went on for many years, later she started to feel it too. Even not, she has suffered this pain on every house. After a few years her situation had become such that she had considered herself a stone, her eyes were sadly falling, but she also used to get dry, no one knew what would happen to her at that time. It was because the impatience used to stay outside the house all the time due to work and that poor man does not say this in the house and does not say this word and after it. After all, what happens next, I do not have the courage that I cannot write that pain in alphabetical order, if I cannot write about everyone, I am feeling so much pain in writing about him, then he has suffered it every time. Every day has been spent in front of the poor poor, trying to escape...) Adheera came to know about this later but she did not say anything bash she said that be a little distant from her, not the poor, but her own daughter, asked her to take her own life. She didn't say anything even when she was silent, because she still had to see the future of your children. He has seen it in front of his eyes, is it nothing, is it nothing, what the sinner has done on him every day, is it nothing? The danger for this is the terrorist of our country, who by eating the filth of our body and taking birth on this earth, has committed this kind of sin. If caught, then the government will keep it in its captivity for a few days, then after that, it will keep it in captivity for a few days, if it is punished, it will also give it to him by feeding it yellow for a year. In the same time she becomes a victim of someone else undefined donation fulfills the truth first. When he started living separately from Adheera's family, then Ahana had also got that he should take revenge for the oppression on himself in some way. .Because his future was very bad. That's why Ahana applied to become police officer . for a few days, after that two or three months after that he got the best rank and he got the best rank in everything. Told that now because she got separated long ago and went to live in the hostel. A few days after the result, her training And after 2 months of that he also took the post of D.P.S. and he also got his posting done in city from where his pain started. He was cut in the middle of the street where his mother Adheera and his brother sister used to live. Do you know what he said to his mother again??????? Had done all this on me, gave me so much pain. So whatever I am today, I can't make it. And one last right I got freedom, I got freedom, my sisters got freedom and that every witness got freedom...if That scoundrel was wrong, so you were wet all the time because even after seeing you did not say anything, but I cannot do anything like this to you... You think about it. Because for me, my whole world is the same. I have slept today. .. impatience in his own eyes. I would never have done it in my whole life. All the moments spent in her past were now being remembered and then she felt that I wish you had raised your voice in front of my father for the first time. Perhaps she would never have been in front of him.

***"'"My luck is my food, my love is my worship.***
***My passion is also there and we write our own destiny.***
***Because we don't trust that God's work***
***I don't know when it was done...."***

# The Egalitarianism

Silence looks as good as long as it doesn't come on you. How many cases are still pending on the police stations, millions of cases are not registered because of someone's silence. We will be defamed and no one will marry our daughter. A woman does not feel alone because there is no one to support her, because she feels alone because in whose shadow she has spent her whole life. When she tells you that you learn to keep quiet, what will she do. There are many such girls who are like disciples. She tries to get justice for herself by breaking the bondage. That's why they are considered as Maa Durga Maa Kali.. But now there are many girls who think about their family and never break their silence against it.. What about those who always think that some gift will come to save us undefined trouble It never happens.. because that time does not come. Everyone thinks that God will save us. because no one is going to save you, but it's true...bash is some last word undefined

*“"Just have to do*
*So let's do that time by which this whole universe is afraid*
*And you want so then choose yourself*
*Cause bigger Problems than you*
*To make you wish of new one......*
*Pull you to the old Memories of yours*
*This is some worship of your beauty*
*This is the story of the whole universe.....*
*when your own society's mess casts a dirty view on some woman*
*I'm a man but I don't care about their veiws*
*I'm a man but, i care*
*When someone is on his own silent even on the oppression*
*i care when one*
*The girl does not understand the pain of the other woman*
*I care because I*
*am also a part of this society*
*I care because*
*I'm a man..."”*

Printed by Libri Plureos GmbH in Hamburg,
Germany